Stillness

52 Weekly Activities
to Rest, Relax, and Embody Wellness

by

Maurya W. Glaude, *Ph.D., M.S.W., L.C.S.W.*

Watersprings
PUBLISHING

Published by Watersprings Publishing,

an imprint of Watersprings Media House, LLC.

P.O. Box 1284 Olive Branch, MS 38654

www.waterspringspublishing.com

Contact the publisher for bulk orders and permission requests.

Printed in the United States of America.

ISBN-13: 978-1-964972-02-2

To Dad

In gratitude for your protection and for teaching us to be grateful and not wasteful. Thank you for the multitude of Sundays when you played outside with us. Thank you for storing your college biology books in the attic. I climbed to gain knowledge.

And, Tim, Xavier, and Kaiya, you inspire me to keep going.

CONTENTS

INTRODUCTION

With all of our commitments and responsibilities, it is common for us to resist being still. We even have advancements in technology like apps and gadgets that message us to move. In a society that's constantly promoting doing and being "on", it's no wonder our bodies are tired, sleep-deprived, and constantly tapping into resilience (or dependent on caffeine). Stillness, therefore seems far out of reach. Yet, stillness is a necessity, not a luxury. Stillness promotes the regulation of our emotions, digestion, and immune functioning. Stillness promotes wellness – physical, mental, and emotional well-being.

Stillness: 52 Weekly Activities to Rest, Relax, and Embody Wellness is a practical guide to stress-reducing and relaxing activities that promote healthy habits and holistic wellness. Unapologetically, these activities were created to teach us to exhale, unwind, and embrace stillness. Keep reading and make a commitment to immerse yourself in wellness, using these 52 weekly activities.

SECTION 1

HEAD-HEART-BODY CONNECTION

Healing Conversations

Our heads and hearts are connected. Within the body's autonomic nervous system is a pair of nerves called the vagus nerves. They run up either side of the neck. These nerves connect the brain with some of our internal organs, including the heart. The vagus nerve also runs from the brain to the gut. The vagus nerves play a key role in regulating our emotions, digestion, and immune function. Therefore, the head-heart-body connection affects everything from physical health to mental and emotional well-being.

When did you last feel like your mind and heart were connected? What habit are you currently practicing that promotes both mental and physical wellness? Are you able to do more of this activity? How often? What are some action steps you currently take to help you increase the frequency of this habit?

Can you commit to repeating this habit weekly? Would using a calendar or app help? Would adding a partner (i.e., accountability partner) help?

The following activities include mantras and mind exercises that promote healing, protect boundaries, and embrace wellness of the mind and body. As you complete each activity, you are reminded to be mindful of your head-heart connection.

Imagine Love, Light, Peace, Courage, and Boundaries

Repeat these words:

"I am love."

"I am light."

"I am peace."

"I am courageous."

"I will set boundaries."

Action step: Commit to repeating these words as many days as possible this week.

Stillness

Moving Closer to Being

Supplies needed:

- *Notepad*

- *Writing utensil*

Using your notepad, write the following prompt:

What kind of thoughts am I having right now?

Place this prompt on your computer monitor or laptop.

Spend time reflecting. Are your thoughts positive?

If your thoughts are positive and productive, protect your energy, and remain positive and productive.

Are your thoughts negative?

If your thoughts are harmful to your wellness, what can you think of to shift your thinking and bring yourself joy or gratitude?

Guide

Morning Mantra

Identify a quote or bible passage that inspires, motivates, or with which you connect. Complete the following:

This week, I strive to… (Write it out)

____

____

____

Say it out loud.

This week I hope to… (Write it out)

____

____

____

Say it out loud.

Stillness

Evening Mantra

Breathe in through your nose and out through your mouth.

Repeat.

Inhale tomorrow. Exhale yesterday.

Breathe in and out. Breathe in and out.

Inhale the confidence of tomorrow's successes.

Exhale the doubts of yesterday.

Breathe in and out. Breathe in and out.

Smile. Bask in the joy of life.

The Power of Saying No Makes Room for Saying Yes

Are you stressed? Are you over-extended and over-committed?

When asked to take on more, have you set boundaries and said no?

Imagine saying no.

Picture yourself saying no.

Say it now:

"No, I cannot." Say: *"No, I cannot until I finish these other priorities."*

Breathe in through your nose and exhale through your mouth.

Remind yourself that you are creating healthier habits and saying no to make room for saying yes.

Stillness

The Power of Saying No
Makes Room for Saying Yes (Continued)

Make a list of the tasks and activities you would like to complete this week (or month, year). Decide whether each item is urgent or not urgent. Place each in the proper column below.

Urgent/Important	Not Urgent/ Not Important	Urgent/ Not Important	Not Urgent/ Not Important

How do you decide whether the task or activity is important or not?

____

____

Does the task help you move forward with your long-term goals?

____

____

Is this someone else's task for me and when is the deadline?

____

____

Can I delegate the task to someone else? If a list is too long, can I break it down into smaller lists and extend the deadlines?

____

____

Stillness

Stillness is a Daily Decision

Each day of the week, say:

"Today, I will choose to embrace stillness."

Action steps:

Choose to slow down, take breaks, and be still.

Wellness Reflection

Are you visiting wellness like it's a relative? Are you living in wellness as a lifestyle? What does your wellness plan look like this week?

Action steps: Create a wellness plan for this week. Consider including activities from *Stillness: 52 Weekly Activities to Rest, Relax, and Embody Wellness*, or add your own activities that include time with friends, healthy meals, Art, Music, reading, photography, gardening, and more! Make an effort to stick to this week of wellness. Try to extend the commitment to two weeks of wellness. Extend your commitment. (See page 70 and make photo copies to use weekly.)

Stillness

The Gift of Living in the Present

This week, how can I be fully present at work?

____

____

____

At home?

____

____

____

With my loved ones?

____

____

____

Guide

The Gift of Living in the Present
(continued)

This week, what are my priorities?

____

____

____

____

Where can I be more focused?

____

____

____

____

Stillness

Revisiting the Simplicity of the Past

Before cell phones and streaming services, we had landlines, stereos, magazines and newspapers, telephone books, and shopped in person for our groceries.

If you revisited the past, how would you spend your time on a Friday evening after school or work?

____

____

How would you start your Saturday morning and with whom would you spend the day?

____

____

What TV show might you watch?

____

____

Now, pretend it's the past, allocate the time to minimize distractions, and simply live in the moment.

____

____

Guide

Sitting Reflection

Where you will sit when you are old shows where you stood in your youth. -Yoruba proverb

Instead of complaining about the world around you, choose to make some changes. When you look back on life, will you be proud of where you once stood?

What are you most proud of?

____

____

What do you wish to accomplish in one year?

Three years?

Five years?

Ten years?

____

____

____

Where do you see yourself sitting when you are old?

____

____

____

Stillness

Celebrate Joyful Moments

Last week, what gave me joy?

____

____

____

____

____

____

____

____

____

____

Release Stress to Make Room for Joy

Last week, what caused me the most stress?

____

____

____

____

What stressors and stress do I need to release?

____

____

____

____

Stillness

Toothbrush Talks with Loved Ones

Yes, intentionally talk during toothbrush time.

1. Ask: "What is one thing that went really well today (or yesterday)?"

2. Ask: "What's one thing that was difficult about today (or yesterday)?"

3. Ask: "What's one thing you want me to know about today (or yesterday, or in general)?"

Discussing something that happened that day or the day before creates community, trust, reliability, and openness with your partner, children, and loved ones.

This is an intentional habit that promotes interdependence. The warmth of these conversations brings healing to the hearts and souls of your partner, children, friends, and you. (Teeth brushing also promotes dental hygiene and heart health).

Guide

Enduring

What is something I want to accomplish this week? What does it take for me to keep going?

____

____

____

____

____

____

____

____

____

____

____

Stillness

Exercising the Mind

When was the last time you read a great blog, article, bible verse, chapter, or book?

____

____

____

What was it about?

____

____

____

In what ways did the reading bring healing to your mind, body, and/or soul?

____

____

____

Guide

SECTION 2

CREATIVITY FOR THE SOUL

Refueling Creativity

Sometimes our creativity fuel gauges run high and other times, low. In these low moments, we need to refuel. Maintaining a steady level of creativity is key to remaining energized and engaged. When we feel our creativity gauge is lower than what our mind, body, and soul desire or need, we may need to color, craft, or find healing through movement and rhythm. The following activities include coloring activities and creative exercises that help us recalibrate, re-tune our vibrations, and with the goal of mimicking stillness.

Refueling Time. Is it time to refuel?

When was the last time you refueled?

____

____

____

What did you do?

____

____

____

What worked well?

____

____

____

What can you do more often?

____

____

____

Stillness

Create Rhythm
by Coloring a Butterfly

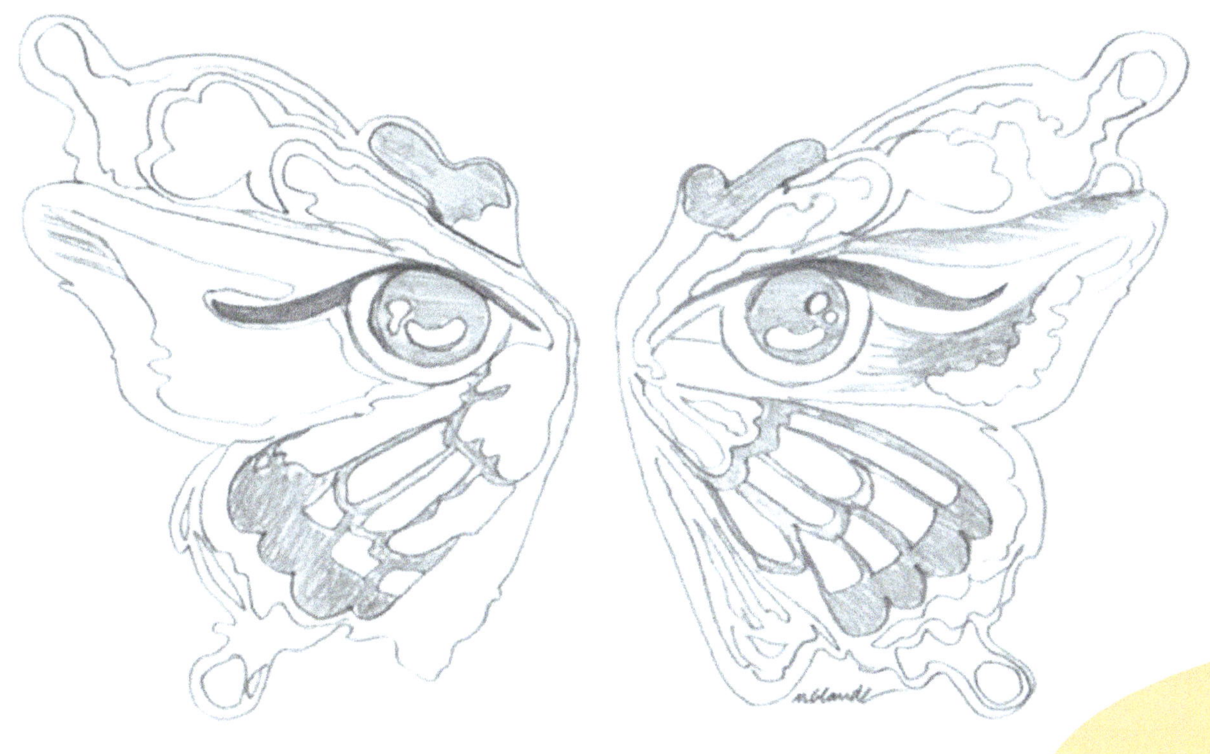

Create Rhythm
by Coloring a Rose

Stillness

Create Rhythm by Creating Inspirational Stone Art

Gather or purchase 2-5" (inch) rocks or stones.

Purchase acrylic pens or acrylic paint and painting brushes, if preferred.

Turn to week one and use a mantra as inspiration or consider a favorite bible verse or inspirational quote for inspiration.

Begin with a background color.

Add a picture and words to your stone. Let your stone dry. Repeat often.

Let's Reset! Reset Recipe

When was the last time you created your own recipe for a reset? What are the perfect ingredients for a cozy night at the house? What are the perfect ingredients for a romantic dinner with your honey? What are the perfect ingredients for a friends' night in the city? What are the perfect ingredients for a stress-releasing girl's day? Spend some time thinking of the perfect ingredients to add to your recipe reset card. Let the ingredients inspire you and add a title.

    a. Schedule the date.

    b. Send out invitations (even if to yourself).

    c. Spend quality time gathering the ingredients.

    d. Enjoy the ingredients and relish in your recipe reset.

Stillness

Making Time for Generational Healing

Select pages from a coloring book or purchase blank or prepped canvasses with paint, crayons, or colored pencils.

Color or draw with your sons, daughters, and senior parents.

Sip lemonade, tea, or fruit juice while creating art with your loved one.

Schedule a second date and send them an electronic or paper invitation to add a little anticipation and joy!

Embrace Rhythm by Coloring a Carnival Mask

Stillness

Envisioning Wellness

What is wellness?

____

____

What does wellness look like in one year?

Five years?

____

____

What are some activities to which I can commit to embody wellness?

____

____

How will I look in one year?

How will my body feel in five years?

____

____

Gather a large sheet of paper like a poster board, glue, scrap paper, scissors, old magazines, markers, and colored pencils. Using these materials, use your creativity and envision wellness.

Guide

Reflecting on a Handful of Successes

With your hands, you make your success. -Yoruba proverb

This week, how will you use your hands to make your success?

____

____

____

____

Stillness

Refueling the Soul

The soul is fueled by love. Love is refueled through an intimate relationship with The Creator. This week, how can you connect with The Creator?

____

____

____

____

SECTION 3

HEALING THROUGH MOVEMENT AND RHYTHM RESETS

Healing Moments

Have you ever gazed at a tree slowly moving in the wind? Did you notice how the gentle breeze and the leaves seemed to dance in slow motion? You see, stillness can also embrace movement. Connecting with a gentle rhythm can help the mind and body slowly reset.

The following activities show appreciation for our senses- touch, smell, sight, hearing, and taste. Through movement like coloring and other creative exercises, we can create a rhythm reset and promote healing within our bodies.

These are Handy!

Look at your hands. Gaze at the lines of your skin. What stories did these hands create?

____

____

Smile at the beautiful melanin.

Smile about the hands that you will hold and the kisses you will blow.

Using a hand, trace the outer thumb with a finger from your other hand. Inhale through your nose to the count of three (3) and exhale to the count of four (4) as you go down and trace the space between your thumb and index finger.

Repeat this tracing, inhaling, and exhaling on the remaining fingers. If tolerated well, add a few drops of essential oils to your hands to enhance the experience.

Stillness

Aromas and Breathing

Have you found a scent that works best to support your reset?

____

____

Does the smell of lavender soothe and calm your anxious energy? ___________

Does cedarwood remind you of the outdoors and help you breathe and slow down your heart rate? _________

Does peppermint give you energy and add a little excitement to your mood?

____

____

Which aromas complement your wellness? What is it about the aroma that relieves, calms, or reduces tension?

____

____

Guide

Bubbles and Kisses Face Yoga

Supplies: Bottle of bubbles and lip balm

Time: 5 or more minutes

First, put some lip balm on your lips. Keeping your lips protected is a great form of self-love.

Next, open your bottle of bubbles. As you blow through the bubble wand, control your breathing, and intentionally create positive thoughts in your mind. For example, think: "I am safe. Breathe in safety through your nose."

Then, as you exhale through your mouth, blow bubbles. Now blow yourself a kiss. Catch it with your hand. (If someone asks what you're doing, tell them you are doing your face yoga!)

As you blow the next set of bubbles, share some bubbles in spaces around your home or office. Visualize safety flowing into these spaces as the bubbles travel through the air. Continue to breathe in safety through your nose while telling yourself that you are safe. Exhale through your mouth. While embracing stillness, allow the bubbles to travel. Follow them with your eyes. Continue to visualize safety as the bubbles travel through the air.

Finally, kiss your hand and then touch your hand to your forehead. Embrace the self-love.

Stillness

Let the Rhythm Move You. Dance!

Have you ever line danced? Do you know the steps to the most famous group line dances? Not only is line dancing great exercise, but it also brings people together.

Search for a line dance using a popular computer search engine.

Invite a family member or friend to join you and let the rhythm move you!

Consider dancing together multiple times this week.

You can even consider joining a line dancing group.

Guide

Mindful Meditation

Meditation is for everyone. Everyone can benefit from meditation. Meditation is not a religion but is a lifestyle. Are you new to meditation?

Have you tried movement meditation like yoga or t'ai chi?

Have you tried breathing meditation or guided meditation?

There is no "right" way to meditate. If you find that thoughts come to your mind during meditation, this is completely normal.

Getting used to meditation takes time.

Have you practiced meditation before?

Try meditation and see if it's a good fit for you.

Stillness

Mindful Meditation (continued)

Sit quietly in a space with natural or dimmed light.

Breathe through your nostrils and exhale through your lips.

Scan the body for sensations and messages starting at your feet and working your way up through your limbs, core, spine, arms, shoulders, neck, and head.

Imagine there's a light (choose your favorite color) or choose the sunlight as the light that scans the body.

Remind the body that it is safe and warm. speak refreshment into the body. Hydrate with water or something warm, like tea.

If tolerated well, add a few drops of essential oils to the palms of your hands. Rub them together and inhale the aroma. Take a few deep breaths in through your nose. Also. add lip balm to your lips to enhance the experience.

Mirroring Mindfulness

As you gaze in the mirror in preparation to wash your face or brush your teeth, intentionally concentrate on the moment.

Clear your mind of your tasks for the day.

Clear your mind of your upcoming work and responsibilities.

Focus on the sound of the water.

Concentrate on the tube of toothpaste in your hand and the softness of the squeeze.

Breathe in the fresh scent of your toothpaste. Notice the rhythm of the brushing.

Cleanse your gums and rinse your mouth. Run your tongue against your teeth and enjoy your clean mouth.

Smile at the person you see in the mirror.

Stillness

Wake up!

This week, wake up a few minutes earlier. Get up. Get dressed and before checking your phone, go outside.

Breathe in some fresh air. If possible, take at least a 3-minute walk. Gaze at the nature around you.

If well tolerated, pick a flower, or touch the bark of a tree. Notice the colors of the leaves.

When you are ready, return home and proceed with your daily routine, awakened by the beauty of nature around you.

Guide

Let the Rhythm 'Mood' You

Creating rhythm in the morning can help you regulate your mood and set the tone for your day.

What song motivates you? What prayer brings you joy? What dance gets you excited? What can you do to keep yourself in a state of positive energy and focused?

(Examples: exercise, meditate, dance, read scripture.)

____

____

____

____

Building Community

IT'S BIGGER THAN ME.

What about my community? Are you part of any organizations?

Have you read the local social media page or newsprint to learn about policies affecting your community?

Are there any local organizations like benevolent or fraternal organizations that share your priorities for the community, i.e., housing, education, and healthcare?

Have you voted your conscience in an election to promote systemic change for housing, education, and healthcare (or another cause) so that you are not always being asked to adapt and demonstrate resilience?

____

____

____

____

Action steps: Identify a community organization. Attend an upcoming activity. Consider joining. Pray about it.

Anxious or Excitement?

Whenever you are anxious about something, could you really be excited? Maybe you are meeting a new friend for the first time. Maybe you are starting a new job. Maybe you are flying on an airplane for the first time or making a major purchase.

Pause and take a few deep breaths.

Inhale through your nose and exhale through your mouth.

Breathe in excitement and exhale anxiety.

Does telling yourself, I must really be excited help you re-frame and channel your anxious energy?

Stillness

Nature Walk

Is there somewhere for you to safely walk in nature?

Choose to take a walk.

Walk with your Creator.

Walk with strength.

Breathe in the fresh air through your nose.

Exhale fear, powerlessness, criticism, and all the toxic negativity as you walk.

Visually appreciate the trees, plants, dirt, animals, and all of nature.

Listen to the water. Listen to the wind. Listen to the quiet.

Allow your vibrations to match the vibrations of nature.

Sunset Reset

When the sun begins to set, the light from the sun passes through the air, and molecules in the atmosphere cause the light rays to scatter.

As a result, we see reds, yellows, blues, and violets, making a marvelously painted sunset.

The colors are refreshing.

Enjoy a sunset and reset.

Reflection: Who Do You See?

When you look in the mirror, who do you see?

____

____

What are the characteristics you possess beneath your melanin-kissed skin?

____

____

Beyond organs, what parts of you would you want to donate?

____

____

____

____

Vintage Moments

Let's take a trip back into time. Recall the year you were born. What's a famous album that was written the year you were born?

____

____

Who's the artist?

____

____

Are you able to relate to any of the artist's lyrics? Which song do you like best?

____

____

Stillness

SECTION 4

JUST ADD WATER!

Holy H$_2$0

Did you know that more than half of the body is made of water? Therefore, you may naturally feel safe in a tub of water or the ocean. You may even feel drawn to the slow trickle of a fountain, stream, or mist on a rainy day. Immersing yourself in water can be renewing and refreshing.

The following includes recipes and activities that encourage relaxation, rest, and rejuvenation to give resilience some rest and promote holistic wellness.

Relaxation Blend: Body Bath Butta.

- 4 cups of plain Epson salts

- 1 cup coarse sea salt (recommend Dead Sea salts can be purchased at many local grocery stores or online)

- 45 drops of your favorite essential oil(s)

- 5 tablespoons of your favorite dried flowers or herbs (i.e., lemongrass, lavender) *crush or chop before adding to the blend.

1. Combine all the ingredients in a large plastic bowl.

2. Be sure to break up any clumps.

3. Scoop your bath salts into an airtight container (i.e., glass jar).

4. Store your salts in a dark and cool place to preserve them.

Guide

Weekly Bath Time

At least once each week, make time for a long calming bath.

Add candles for aroma and lighting.

Listen to the water as it fills the tub.

Instead of scrolling through your phone, add calming water sounds and relax for a while.

Let the water soothe your muscles.

Stillness

Rain, Rain, Come, and Let's Pray!

Have you sat quietly to relax on a rainy day?

What rhythm does the rain make as it falls to the earth?

What are the aromas that you smell?

Like our bodies, much of the earth is water, and therefore, rainwater is needed to refresh Mother Earth. We even witness animals preparing for rain and the abundance that water brings.

In what ways do you prepare for rain?

____

____

Action step: Select a prayer to recite for the next rainy day. When it rains, remember to pray.

Planting the Seeds of Wellness

Do you garden? Do you have houseplants?

Not only do plants purify the air, they may have medicinal properties that help you lower your stress. House plants are natural air purifiers and many prefer drier conditions. Others have anti-inflammatory properties.

What type of plant would fit well in your home?

____

____

Action steps: Shop for your plant. Add it to your favorite room or even your office. Nurture your plant by watering it regularly and add vitamins as needed.

Stillness

Prepare for Rain

The next time it's about to rain, embrace the stillness.

Prepare. Choose to sit quietly and listen to the raindrops.

Later, reflect.

How do you feel in your mind, heart, stomach?

____

____

____

Prepare for Rain
(continued)

Identify two or more ways you showed your mind love last week.

____

____

____

Identify one or more ways you showered your heart with kindness in the last few days.

____

____

____

Identify two or more ways you showed your stomach self-care today.

____

____

____

Stillness

It's Time to Spill the Tea

Are you harboring old hurts with a friend or loved one? Invite them over for tea time or meet at the local coffee house.

Purchase your favorite tea. (My favorite is organic green tea because of its healthy properties.)

- Sip your tea.

- Spill the tea (not literally!) *Apologize.*

- Accept your wrongness.

- Give them time to respond and react (even if they are not ready to forgive you).

- Listen fully to hear (and not to respond).

- Ask for forgiveness.

- Forgive yourself.

- Commit to peace.

Laugh Until You Cry

Laughter heals.

Choose a favorite old comedy or find a new favorite.

Laugh until you cry.

Action steps: In the next two weeks, watch a movie at the cinema or visit a comedy show.

Stillness

Is Your Wellness Faucet Turned On?

Does your wellness plan drip?

Does your wellness plan pour?

Is your wellness faucet even turned on?

Action steps: What are three activities you can commit to completing in the next two weeks? Develop a wellness plan for the week.

____

____

____

____

____

____

____

____

____

Clean Up Your Life

Just Add Water with lemon or lavender!

Cleaning and decluttering can activate a sense of accomplishment. Lemon awakens and lavender calms.

Do you already have lemon or lavender-scented cleaning products?

Do you have a lemon or lavender candle?

Pick a small area of your home that needs your attention and clean up! Use lemon or lavender scents to complement the cleaning.

Stillness

IT'S OKAY TO GET PROFESSIONAL HELP.

If you're dealing with a lot and you need additional help with managing stress, grief, anxiety, depressed mood, or other mental health symptoms, seek out the assistance of a licensed clinical social worker, psychologist, professional counselor, or other mental health professionals. Try calling the number on your health insurance card or contact your human resources department to discuss confidential services, like EAP benefits. You can also try dialing 211 (24-hour mental health and referral services), 988 (24-hour Crisis Lifeline), or 866-903-3787 (National Mental Health Hotline).

Guide

WEEKLY PLANNER

Monday

Tuesday

Wednesday

Thursday

Friday

Saturday

Sunday

Stillness

For more support in your wellness journey, purchase the companion book **Stillness: Habits to maintain mental wellness and give *Resilience* a break.**

Paperback ISBN: 978-1-964972-01-5
Available everywhere books are sold.

www.ingramcontent.com/pod-product-compliance
Lightning Source LLC
La Vergne TN
LVHW081936060225
802923LV00016B/598